Growing Your Love After The "I Do's" God's Way Workbook

Dr. Shameka Mack Sanders

© 2017 Dr. Shameka Mack Sanders
All rights reserved.

ISBN: 0998910228

ISBN 13: 978-0998910222

Sanders Publications LLC

Contents

Session One 13
    Chapter 1 God's Plan Not Mine Questions 15
Session Two 25
    Chapter 2 The Wedding Day Questions 27
Session Three 33
    Chapter 3 Fake It Till You Make It or Not Questions 35
Session Four 49
    Chapter 4 Enough is Enough Questions 51
Session Five 63
    Chapter 5 The Truth Heals Questions 65
Session Six 71
    Chapter 6 Loving Your Spouse Questions 73
Session Seven 83
    Chapter 7 Growing Your Love God's Way Questions 85
Session Eight 89
    Chapter 8 Tips For Growing Your Love God's Way Questions 91

GETTING STARTED

Welcome to the *Growing Your Love After The "I Do's" God's Way Workbook*. The journey you are about to embark on will help you grow your love and rebuild your marriage by discovering and applying the *best* strategies for having a happy, healthy, and successful marriage. Dr. Sanders has provided you with thought-provoking strategies in this workbook and in the accompanying book, *Growing Your Love After The "I Do's" God's Way* that will aid you and your spouse as you begin this life-changing journey.

Dr. Sanders explains, in this book, with raw honesty, how marriages built on weak foundations and selfishness can become troubled. She also underscores God's plan for marriage and offers credible evidence that when you marry *God's way*, you deliberately choose love and commitment over selfishness. Moreover, you are provided with valuable information and tools throughout the book that helps you grow your love *God's way*. In addition, this workbook provides you with a private place (for both you and your spouse) to complete a variety of exercises, identify the issues in your marriage, discuss hard truths, and begin the process of using Dr. Sanders's strategies as a catalyst to rebuilding your marriage and growing your love.

The workbook and book were designed to be used together and is for couples committed to growing their love and rebuilding their marriage. In addition, they both can be used to help individuals determine if they are truly ready for the life-long commitment of marriage.

But, before starting the journey, here are a few tips that will help you throughout the process:

- ✓ **Tip 1: Recognize this journey, as a marathon, *not* a sprint**

    It is important to take your time, as you embark on this new journey. Given that it took time for your marriage to become dysfunctional, it will take time to rebuild it. There is no need to rush through the process, just to say you completed the journey. Rather, give yourself time to evaluate, discuss, and implement the information provided in this workbook. Also, give yourself time to focus on the areas that really speak to the needs of you and your spouse. Remember: You do not have to cover all of the sessions at once, or even answer all the questions. If you find an area that you and your spouse are doing well in, discuss it briefly, and move on. After all, this workbook is designed to help grow your love *God's way*, while you develop a better relationship with Him.

- ✓ **Tip 2: Come ready to learn and be open and honest with yourself and your spouse**

    This is the time to listen to your spouse, learn what he/she needs from you, acknowledge the actions that got you to this point, eliminate defensiveness, and most importantly, seek God's knowledge, wisdom, and understanding. *Start every session with expectations.* In other words, *expect* that if you put forth the maximum effort, outlined in this workbook, with an honest and open mind, allowing God to guide you, you will be on the *right* path to growing your love and rebuilding your marriage. Most importantly, put an *expectation* on your faith by expecting *God to work.* Note: Each session is filled with biblical scriptures to help you build your faith and develop a closer relationship with God and your spouse. And, although there is no one-size-fits-all plan for growing your love and rebuilding your marriage, know that this journey is designed to help you learn more about your marriage, so you can truly understand what works best for you, your spouse, and your marriage.

✓ **Tip 3: Respect your spouse**

It is essential that you *respect* your spouse. More specifically, *respect* his/her feelings, perspective, and truth. Throughout this process, you will encounter questions that cause you and/or your spouse to become vulnerable, due to the sensitivity of the issue being discussed. When this happens and tension rise, either take a moment to gather your thoughts or table the discussion for another time. However, *do not* overlook the discussion, as it will be vital to the growth of your marriage. Plus, if you and your spouse both feel respected, the tension will slowly dissipate. Therefore, patience, forgiveness, consistency, and a judgement-free zone should be at the forefront, as you embark on this life-changing journey.

✓ **Tip 4: Work with your spouse and *not* against your spouse**
Recognize that your spouse is really your *ally* - not your *enemy*. Note: If you continue to work against your spouse, you will limit your ability to experience the "oneness" with your spouse that God intended.

✓ **Tip 5: Understand the true purpose of the workbook**
You can complete this journey, as an individual, or with your spouse. If your spouse is not ready to take this journey with you, you can *still* reap the benefits of this profound journey without him/her. The questions in this book are designed for both individuals and couples. However, as you begin to apply the principles of the *Growing Your Love Journey* on a consistent basis, your spouse may decide to "get in on the action." In this workbook, you'll find both general questions and questions specifically for couples. You should answer the general questions first, then the questions that apply to your gender. In addition to the general questions and gender-specific questions, couples should answer the questions designated for him and her:

For Him: Questions for husbands
For Her: Questions for wives
For Him and Her: Questions for husbands and wives

A Message from Dr. Sanders

Again, welcome to the *Growing Your Love Journey*. And, if you're wondering if this journey is going to be another failed attempt at growing your love and rebuilding your marriage… DON'T. Speaking from experience, the information provided in the *Growing Your Love After The "I Do's" God's Way* book will not only help you discover God's plan for marriage, but also help you rebuild your marriage with a strong foundation – a foundation strengthened by God's love.

The truth is when a marriage is damaged, dysfunctional, and/or demolished, restoration needs to take place, through the process of rebuilding, which, let's be honest, takes hard work, consistency, patience, and most importantly - God's help. Now, I understand that some days you will most likely feel "tapped out," thus, progress will seem out of your reach, but do not stop working - keep going! The breakthrough at the end of your journey is worth every bit of discomfort you may experience while going through the process. Remember, *you can do all things through Christ* (Philippians 4:13). And, the results from your "rebuilding efforts" will be more beautiful than anything you've ever experienced.

Are you ready to embark on this life-changing journey? You can do this! Let's get started!

SESSION ONE

Session One (Chapter One) covers *God's Plan Not Mine*. In this chapter, Dr. Sanders discusses God's plan for marriage (evidenced through bible principles). She also explores how *selfish ways* can prevent individuals from experiencing God's plan for marriage. As an example, Dr. Sanders explains how her own *selfishness* contributed to her troubled marriage. Therefore, the questions in this session were designed to help you identify important factors that have caused you and your spouse to drift towards isolation in your relationship, thereby, leading to the neglect of the wants and needs of your spouse. To prepare for this session: Read Chapter One prior to starting the session. Also remember, to answer the general questions first and the gender-related questions, second. Couples should answer the questions designated for him and her, last.

The scriptures accompanying this section are:

Hebrews 13:4
Genesis 2:18-24
Matthew 19:6
Malachi 2:13-16
Jeremiah 17:9
Proverbs 28:26
James 3:8

Proverbs 18:21
Proverbs 15:2
Ecclesiastes 10:12
Romans 8:17
Ephesians 2:18
Philippians 2:13
Colossians 1:11

*If you need additional space to answer the questions, or would like to journal your thoughts, please refer to the "Notes Section" in Appendix A.

Chapter One
God's Plan Not Mine
Questions

In Chapter One, Dr. Sanders discusses God's plan for marriage, while explaining how marriage is *not* just a ceremony. She goes further in explaining that God does not intend for couples to divorce, and that *His* ultimate plan for marriage is to reflect *His* image and provide the world with a picture of *His* love.

What is your understanding of God's plan for marriage?

_____
_____
_____
_____
_____
_____
_____
_____
_____
_____
_____
_____
_____
_____
_____
_____
_____

Have you truly received your spouse, as God's gift to you, and do you view your spouse as someone, who can and should be replaced?

_____
_____
_____
_____
_____
_____
_____
_____
_____
_____
_____
_____

Write down a few things that you are thankful for, in regards to your spouse?

_____
_____
_____
_____
_____

_____
_____
_____
_____
_____
_____
_____

What is preventing you from receiving your spouse, as God's special gift to you?

_____
_____
_____
_____
_____
_____
_____
_____
_____
_____

On pg. 17, Dr. Sanders explains that some couples chose divorce because they are selfish. They underestimate the amount of work needed to make a marriage work. As a result, some of the questions she poses are: What about *me*?" or "What about the things *I* want to do?" or "What about what *I* need?"

Have you found yourself asking these questions? If not these particular questions, which questions have you asked yourself that have caused you to put your needs and desires above your spouse's?

_____
_____
_____
_____
_____
_____
_____
_____
_____
_____
_____

Would you categorize yourself as a selfish individual? Why or Why Not?

_____
_____
_____
_____
_____

For Him: What actions have you displayed that have caused you to be selfish toward your wife?

For Her: What actions have you displayed that have caused you to be selfish towards you husband?

_____
_____
_____
_____
_____
_____
_____
_____
_____
_____
_____
_____

For Him and Her: Discuss your responses together. Be sure to respect your spouse by striving to understand his/her feelings, perspectives, and truths.

On pg. 19, Dr. Sanders discuss the consequences of depending on feelings. Your feelings play a colossal role in the drift towards isolation in your relationship.

How has depending on your feelings impacted your marriage?

_____
_____
_____

___

___

___

___

___

___

___

___

___

___

___

For Him: In comparison to the time you and your spouse first married, how have you drifted away from your wife?

___

___

___

___

___

___

___

___

___

___

___

___

___

___

For Her: In comparison to the time you and your spouse first married, how have you drifted away from your husband?

_____
_____
_____
_____
_____
_____
_____
_____
_____
_____
_____

For Him: What areas do you think you and your spouse need to work on, so you do not drift away from her?

_____
_____
_____
_____
_____
_____
_____

For Her: What areas do you think you and your spouse need to work on, so you do not drift away from him?

For Him and Her: Discuss and evaluate your responses. Share ideas on what you can do to better reconnect with your spouse. This will help you focus on what you can do better *not* on what your spouse needs to do. Responses to these questions may be sensitive for some. If they are, take your time in this section and allow yourselves to really evaluate and discuss the issues that have caused you to drift away from your spouse.

Dear Father,
I believe your ultimate plan for marriage is to not only reflect your image, but also provide the world with a true picture of love. Father, your Word says, "Husbands and wives are to walk in oneness." So, I ask you to help my spouse and I walk in oneness. Help us to be less selfish and more selfless. In Jesus Name, Amen.

SESSION TWO

Session Two covers Chapter Two, *The Wedding Day*. In preparation for this session, read Chapter Two, in its entirety. In this chapter, Dr. Sanders discusses the excitement and preparation of planning a wedding, while failing to admit to herself and her soon-to-be-spouse that she really was not ready for marriage. She then goes even further to explain how relationships built on a weak foundation are *not* able to support a healthy marriage. Therefore, the goal of these questions are to help you better identify the strength of your marital foundation. Remember, answer the general questions first, and then the questions that pertain to your specific gender. In addition to the general questions and gender specific questions, couples should answer the questions designated for him and her.

The scripture accompanying this section is:

1 Thessalonians 4:3-5

*If you need additional space to answer the questions or would like to journal your thoughts, please refer to the "Notes Section" in Appendix B.

Chapter Two
The Wedding Day
Questions

On pg. 25, Dr. Sanders discusses an experience that occurred on her wedding day. On pg. 26, she says, "Oftentimes, people get married for the wrong reasons, then they either wind up in a healthy marriage or in a troubled union that is on the verge of divorce."

What is your viewpoint on this statement?

___

For Him: What made you decide to marry your wife?

___

For Her: What made you decide to marry your husband?

For Him and Her: Compare your answers with your spouse. Determine if your thoughts and actions have helped build a solid foundation for your marriage - a foundation with God at the forefront of your marriage.

On a scale of 1-10 with 10 being the highest, how big of a role do you desire God to play in your marriage?

When building a strong foundation in your marriage, it is important to have a spiritual relationship with God. Why? Well, because marriage works best when you and your spouse are individually connected to God. Therefore, ask yourself these questions:

Did I allow myself to be an integral part of God's family, before building my own? If so, how?

_____
_____
_____
_____
_____
_____
_____
_____
_____
_____
_____
_____

Can I honestly say that my spouse and I have given God total control of our lives and are allowing Him to guide our marriage? If so, how?

_____
_____
_____
_____
_____
_____
_____
_____
_____
_____

What have you done personally to ensure that you are on the *right* path to building a spiritual foundation in your marriage? Check all that apply.

____ Spend alone time with God
____ Study the Bible together
____ Pray for your spouse
____ Pray with your spouse
____ Attach yourself to a church home

For Him: What are some steps you can take to ensure you are on the *right* path to building a spiritual foundation in your marriage?

___

For Her: What are some steps you can take to ensure you are on the *right* path to building a spiritual foundation in your marriage?

_____

_____

_____

_____

_____

For Him and Her: Compare and discuss your answers. You will learn a lot about how your spouse views your relationship. In fact, once Dr. Sanders discovered that her marriage was standing on a weak foundation, and confessed her truths, as to why she truly married, she and her husband, Clifton, were able to begin the process of rebuilding their marriage on a spiritual foundation, strengthened by God's love.

Father,
I pray right now for my marriage. Teach my spouse and me how to depend on your power so that the foundation of our marriage can be strengthened. Mature and refine us both so that we can be motivated by compassion, love, and grace. Father, I want more for my marriage. So, I ask you to infuse my marriage with the passion to grow. In Jesus Name, Amen.

SESSION THREE

Session Three covers Chapter Three, *Fake It Till You Make It or Not*. In this chapter, Dr. Sanders discusses how past experiences can impact your marriage. More specifically, distorted thoughts about marriage and parenting are examined in this chapter to help you get a better understanding of what prevents people from overcoming life challenges. In addition, she talks about having a 'single mom' mentality, while being married. Pretending to be a loving and happily married couple in public, but being miserable behind closed doors is also highlighted in this chapter. She goes even further and details how she had to admit that her marriage was in trouble and seek God for help in order to save it. In preparation for this session, read Chapter Three, in its entirety. Remember, answer the general questions first, and then the questions that pertain to your specific gender. In addition to the general questions and gender specific questions, couples should answer the questions designated for him and her.

The scriptures accompanying this section are:

Romans 12:2
Ezekiel 18:31
Proverbs 3:5-6
James 2:26
James 2:21-22
Ephesians 5:21-33
Colossians 3:18

Proverbs 31:10-12
James 4:17
Philippians 4:6-7
Isaiah 55:11
Hebrews 10:38
Matthew 6:33

*If you need additional space to answer the questions, please refer to the "Notes Section" in Appendix C. Also, do not forget to journal your thoughts on this section.

Chapter Three
Fake It Till You Make It or Not Questions

This chapter begins on pg. 31. It touches on the time after the wedding, when family and friends have left, and reality has begun to set in – the time when we are left with only each other and any children in the mix. That is when the real work begins. It is important to recognize, realize, and understand that marriage is *not* just a ceremony, but a commitment that requires hard work, and a lot of effort from both parties.

In marriage there are good times, bad times, and really hard times; however, you must remember that marriage is a promise, *not* a contract. What are your thoughts about this statement? Do you think you are required to make additional efforts to keep your marriage happy and healthy? Please explain.

_____

_____

_____

_____

_____

_____

_____

_____

_____

_____

_____

_____

For Him and Her: Discuss your answers with your spouse. Take your time, when answering this question, as this question is designed to help you and your spouse get a better understanding of each other's ideas and marriage expectations. If you struggle with communication, this question will help you "get the ball rolling," thus, opening up the lines of communication, so you can begin identifying areas of concern and building a stronger foundation for your marriage. Refrain from arguing with your spouse due to his/her responses, and try to understand his/her perspectives.

In addition, Dr. Sanders discusses her desires to "give up" on her marriage on pg. 32. In Session Two, you were asked to discuss some of the things that are causing you to drift away from your marriage and spouse. Have you "given up" on your marriage and spouse? Be honest with yourself, as your answer to this question will determine how much work you need to do to grow your love.

- ☐ Yes
- ☐ No

If you answered "No" to this question, that's great! And, if you answered "Yes" to this question, that's "Ok" too! It's *differences* and *selfishness*, as discussed in Chapter One, that cause couples to "give up" on their marriages. However, it's the *Word of God* that helps you change your thoughts, and it's walking by the Holy Spirit that helps bring about your healing and restoration. So, if you take this journey serious, and put in the necessary effort for growing your love and rebuilding your marriage, then your "Yes" will turn into a "No."

On pg. 33, Dr. Sanders discusses her personal experiences in the dismissal of her husband and marriage. How have you neglected your spouse?

_____

_____

_____

How has your inaction impacted your marriage?

For Him: List five ways you can give more attention to your wife? If you want to list more than five ways, feel free to do so.

1.

2.

3.

4.

5.

For Her: List five ways you can give more attention to your husband. If you want to list more than five ways, feel free to do so.

1.

2.

3.

4.

5.

For Him and Her: Work diligently throughout the week to implement your responses and discuss your observations at the beginning of Session Four.

One of the questions posed on pg. 34 is "How does someone fix 'something,' when he/she doesn't know a problem even exists?" Well, because your spouse is *not* a "mind reader," it is extremely important to communicate when you have issues because communication is essential to growing your love and building a stronger foundation.

What issues have you communicated to your spouse?

_____
_____
_____
_____
_____
_____
_____
_____
_____
_____
_____
_____

What issues have you not communicated, but need to?

_____
_____

_____
_____
_____
_____
_____
_____
_____
_____
_____
_____
_____

For Him and Her: This may be a very sensitive topic, which is why the above questions were designed to *force* you to identify and discuss the perpetual "elephant in the room" that is causing the breakdown in your marriage.

Dr. Sanders asserts on pg. 35 that she originally *ignored* and/or *refused* to hear God's Word, which prevented it from being properly planted in her. Remember, the key to a successful marriage is growth. Once Dr. Sanders allowed God's plan for marriage to manifest in her own marriage, she experienced a "rebirth" of her commitment to her husband.

For Him: What *actions* are preventing the growth of your marriage? Focus on your own actions, and refrain from pointing fingers to make a point and/or highlight your wife's actions.

_____
_____
_____

For Her: What *actions* are preventing the growth of your marriage? Focus on your own actions, and refrain from pointing fingers to make a point and/or highlight your husband's actions.

For Him and Her: Are you aware of the importance of communicating, and *not* neglecting your spouse's wants and needs? FYI: No spouse wants to feel ignored; therefore, it is important to *willingly* allow the Holy Spirit to guide you.

On pg. 38, Dr. Sanders talks about how love is transitional. In fact, she refers to love, as something that is learned. *It is not just a feeling.* Do you view love, as a sacrifice? How?

_____
_____
_____
_____
_____
_____
_____
_____
_____
_____
_____
_____

For Him and Her: Discuss your response to this question with your spouse and determine some ways, in which you and your spouse can improve in this area.

Truth: We all have 'something' in our marriages that we hide from the world - something that prevents our marriages from growing? What is preventing you and your spouse from building a continual bond and growing your love (i.e. pretending to be happy, committing adultery, having children outside of the marriage....the list goes on and on)?

_____
_____
_____
_____
_____
_____
_____
_____
_____
_____
_____
_____

On pgs. 40-43, Dr. Sanders discusses the concepts of leaving, cleaving, and submission. These concepts are the hallmarks of growing your love *God's way*.

"Leaving" is defined as the shifting of loyalties from others to each other, and "cleaving" is defined as building a relational bond. What are your viewpoints on these two concepts? Refer to *Genesis 2:24* for help. Have you truly embraced the "leave" and "cleave" concepts in your marriage? If so, in what ways?

_____
_____
_____

God designed different, but equal roles and responsibilities for husbands and wives. These roles are outlined in *Ephesians 5:21–33*, *Colossians 3:18*, and *Proverbs 31:10–12*. How do you view your role, as a husband or wife?

___

___

___

For Him: I love and lead my wife by…

___

___

___

___

___

___

___

___

___

___

___

For Her: I respect and follow (support) my husband by…

___

___

___

___

___

_____
_____
_____
_____
_____
_____
_____
_____

On pg. 45, Dr. Sanders explores the "vicious cycle." The "vicious cycle" occurs when you and your spouse are on a "merry-go-round" of repetition. In other words, you keep doing the same things, expecting different results. Because you have placed a Band-Aid on your issues, instead of ascertaining how to fix them, the "merry-go-round" continues to spin. The truth is the only way to slow or stop the "merry-go-round" is to address and fix the problems. Once you resolve your issues (or at least come to a healthy compromise), you can grow your marriage *God's way*. Describe the "vicious cycle" in your marriage.

_____
_____
_____
_____
_____
_____
_____
_____

_____

_____

_____

_____

If you have not transcended beyond your emotions, thus, allowing yourself to fully receive what God has already 'predestined' for your marriage, then you are allowing the "vicious cycle" to wreak havoc on your relationship. Therefore, on a scale of 1-10, how much "fight" to do have left in order to slow the "merry-go-round" and stop the "vicious cycle?"

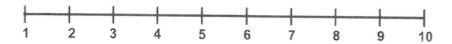

Truthfully, you simply need to be "willing." In other words, the *only* way to get off the "merry-go-round" is to work with your spouse - not against him/her.

In this chapter, Dr. Sanders discusses how she dismissed the Word of God, turning to the World instead to guide her decision-making skills when it came to her marriage. FYI: People sometimes find themselves *unintentionally* turning away from God, because of their situations. What is your viewpoint on this statement? How has your marriage grown by doing this?

_____

_____

_____

_____

_____

_____

Heavenly Father,

Thank you for my marriage. Protect me and my spouse against the "evils" that threaten both our faith and marriage. Father, open our hearts, so we can be more submissive towards each other, and fulfill our responsibilities as husband and wife, the way you designed. In Jesus Name, Amen.

SESSION FOUR

Session Four covers Chapter Four, *Enough is Enough*. In this chapter, Dr. Sanders delves into the concept of "pretending to have a happy, healthy marriage." This chapter will help you learn that it simply is *not* enough to "pretend" to be happy. The key to marital happiness is to develop a strong relationship with God, truly understand His word, and surround yourself with other couples, who strive to follow God's plan for marriage. Thus, the importance of life choices are throughout the chapter with the goal of demonstrating how your responses to situations are critical for success. In preparation for this session, read Chapter Four, in its entirety. Remember, answer the general questions first, and then the questions that pertain to your specific gender. In addition to the general questions and gender specific questions, couples should answer the questions designated for him and her.

The scriptures accompanying this section are:

Galatians 6:9
Isaiah 40:31
Corinthians 5:7
Corinthians 5:17
Jeremiah 29:11

Jeremiah 6:14
Psalms 30:2
Psalms 147:3
Ephesians 4:32
Matthew 6:14-15

*If you need additional space to answer the questions, please refer to the "Notes Section" in Appendix C. Also, do not forget to journal your thoughts on this section.

Chapter Four
Enough is Enough
Questions

Dr. Sanders opens this chapter by stating "In the process of 'pretending' to be something I was not, I lost myself and my happiness. I did not love myself, let alone my spouse. I had lied about the condition of my marriage for so long that I became out-of-touch with reality." 'Pretending' is a form of denial, which can have negative consequences on your marriage. Has 'pretending' impacted your marriage? If so, how?

_____
_____
_____
_____
_____
_____
_____
_____
_____
_____
_____
_____
_____
_____
_____

For Him: What issues have you "swept under the rug," pretending they do not exist?

_____
_____
_____
_____
_____
_____
_____
_____
_____
_____
_____

For Her: What issues have you "swept under the rug," pretending they do not exist?

_____
_____
_____
_____
_____
_____
_____

___

___

___

___

___

___

___

For Him and Her: Discuss your answers with your spouse. The more open and honest you are about the issues in your marriage, the better you can address them.

On pgs. 52-53, the concept of "negative thoughts" is explored to demonstrate how these thoughts can impact every area of your life. Ultimately, how you think is a *choice* - a choice that involves the conscious effort of *choosing* to allow faith to guide your thought processes. So, take a moment to evaluate your thought process, when it comes to your marriage, and, then ask yourself, "Are my decisions truly made in faith, or are they really based on fear, frustration, and dishonesty?

___

___

___

___

___

___

___

___

For Him: How do you respond to issues in your marriage, and how effective have your responses been?

For Her: How do you respond to issues in your marriage, and how effective have your responses been?

_____
_____
_____
_____
_____
_____
_____
_____
_____
_____

For Him and Her: Discuss your responses with your spouse and determine how you and your spouse would like to improve/change the way you respond to things in your marriage. FYI: *Unresolved issues can quickly lead to anger.* Moreover, anger ignored or dismissed can lead to destruction. To break the pattern of dysfunctional decision-making, analyze your decisions, confess misdeeds (according the Word of God), and await God's response.

On pgs. 54-55, the importance of identifying *why* certain people are in your life is discussed. According to Dr. Sanders, "God placed the "right" people in my life, so they could show me how "believers" are *supposed* to walk." Therefore, when surrounding yourself with other married couples, who have God at the center of their marriages, ask them how they managed to maintain strong marriages, and then pay close attention to how they speak and interact with each other. Note: Refrain from surrounding yourself with individuals, who always complain about their spouse.

How are the people in your life helping you "better" your marriage?

_____
_____

Also, in this chapter, Dr. Sanders placed a lot of focus on "I" statements, rather than "You" statements to express the steps taken to respect her husband. *To husbands*, a lack of respect leads to "cold/devoid of love" responses to your wives. *To wives*, a lack a love leads to disrespectful responses to your husbands. This sentiment is highlighted in Ephesians 5:21-33. FYI: All too often, couples participate in "vicious cycles," as discussed in the previous section, and, as a result, they do not realize that their actions are hurting their spouses and causing them to drift apart from each other. Therefore, it is important to evaluate your actions, so you can recognize how your actions are making your spouse feel unloved and disrespected.

For Him: Focus on "I" statements here. For example, "As a husband I feel disrespected when…and I often respond by…

1.

2.

3.

4.

For Her: Focus on "I" statements here. For example, "As a wife I feel unloved when…and I often respond by…

1.

2.

3.

4.

For Him: The next time I feel disrespected by my wife, I can…

_____
_____
_____
_____
_____
_____
_____
_____

For Her: The next time I feel unloved by my husband, I can...

For Him and Her: Be gentle and sensitive, when discussing your responses in this section. Take a few minutes to pray with your spouse, before this discussion. Then, reaffirm your love and respect for each other. Document any "light bulb moments" you experienced in this section.

How has your spouse's treatment of you impacted the way you treat him/her?

Dr. Sanders explore the concept of "making a commitment to walk by faith" (for real, for real) on pgs. 56-58. She also made the statement, "I was desperate, and this desperation called for desperate prayers and actions." How are your actions "lining up" with your commitment to rebuild your marriage and grow your love?

_____
_____
_____
_____
_____
_____
_____

Have your marital issues caused you to question God's ability to restore your marriage and grow your love. If so, explain how you have turned away from God, when it comes to growing your love.

- ☐ Yes
- ☐ No

_____
_____
_____
_____
_____
_____
_____
_____

On pg. 60, Dr. Sanders makes an important statement, "I was still harboring hurt in my heart, which prevented me from spiritually growing and healing." This statement is essential to understanding how to truly restore your marriage and grow your love. Note: When trying to restore your marriage and grow your love, the first step is to be honest with yourself and your spouse.

How many times have you said, "I'm over it!" or "I'm good!" Did those issues continue to resurface in your marriage, and if so, why?

_____
_____
_____
_____
_____
_____
_____
_____
_____
_____
_____
_____

For Him and Her. Compare responses with your spouse. The responses may make you feel vulnerable; however, the benefits of this discussion are well worth it the discomfort.

Dear Father,

I thank you for unconditional love. Help my spouse and me make choices that will solidify our marriage. Help us live out your Word consistently. Father, we invite you into our marriage. Remove the burden of pain, frustration, resentment, bitterness, and anger, and replace them with hope, love, happiness, grace, trust, and forgiveness. Provide us with the courage needed to successfully fulfill your plan for marriage, and the wisdom needed to see the light when the darkness surrounds us. In Jesus Name, Amen.

SESSION FIVE

Congratulations! You are halfway through the *Growing Your Love Journey*. So far you have been introduced to God's plan for marriage, discussed the foundation of your marriage, learned about the "vicious cycle," and addressed issues that you have ignored in your marriage. Going forward you will dig a little deeper, as you embark on the journey of communicating your truths, understanding how to love your spouse *God's way*, and exercising eleven life-changing tips to growing your love. In Session Five, we will examine the topic of healing, specifically, *The Truth Heals*. Note: This session is short; however, it is also powerful and essential for your marital growth. It was designed to explore any issues/concerns you may have suppressed. To prepare for this session, read Chapter Five, in its entirety. Chapter Five involves addressing the *real* reason behind the pain, anger, and frustration in your marriage. The goal is to be completely honest, even if you have terrifying fears of doing so. According to Dr. Sanders, although being honest (no matter what) is *challenging*, it is a critical part of healing and growing your love *God's way*. Remember, answer the general questions first, and then the questions that pertain to your specific gender. In addition to the general questions and gender specific questions, couples should answer the questions designated for him and her.

The scriptures accompanying this section are:

Isaiah 41:10
2 Timothy 1:7
Ephesians 4:32

1 Corinthians 7:3-5
John 8:32
Psalms 34:18

James 5:16

*Continue to journal your thoughts and any notes in Appendix E. In addition, at this point in the journey, what are your current thoughts about your marriage? How do you feel this journey is impacting your marriage?

CHAPTER FIVE
THE TRUTH HEALS
QUESTIONS

Everyone has a *"truth"* to tell. Nevertheless, it is imperative to understand that communicating your "truth" to your spouse takes place on two distinct levels: content ("truth") and relational (love). Dr. Sanders begins Chapter Five (on pg. 63) by explaining how "vocalizing my 'truth' to my husband was one of the most challenging, yet essential things I have ever done, in regards to my marriage." What are your thoughts about this statement and why do you think telling your "truth" about your marriage is essential to your growth?

_____
_____
_____
_____
_____
_____
_____
_____
_____
_____
_____
_____
_____
_____

The ideology of *fear* is discussed on pgs. 63-64. *Fear has a tendency to paralyze progression.* If you are operating in fear in any area of your marriage, you are preventing growth.

Fear of divorce, loving your spouse enough, the unknown, distance, fighting, resentment, frustration, lack of communication, bitterness, etc. are all among the *fears* in marriage. In what ways or areas have you allowed *fear* to stop you from "bettering" your marriage?

_____
_____
_____
_____
_____
_____
_____
_____
_____
_____
_____

What can you do in the next couple of days to prevent *fear* from stopping your marital growth?

_____
_____
_____
_____
_____

On pgs. 73-74, Dr. Sanders explains that "the act of speaking my 'truth' was a catalyst for my healing. Confessing my 'truth' and breaking my silence on my marital issues were a part of God's plan for my healing."

When the *real* issue is not being addressed, communicating your "truth" is critical. Therefore, as you and your spouse begin to reveal your past, present, and future plans, you'll become more equipped to make decisions that will "better" your marriage, such as validating each other's feelings. This action helps you and your spouse tap into your compatibility, because your hearts are healing, strongholds are being broken, burdens are being lifted, and decisions are being made that work well for both of you – at the same time.

What "truth(s)" are holding you hostage and preventing you from rebuilding your marriage and growing your love God's way?

Have you been completely transparent in your marriage (sharing what is true and real to you and being open to each other and unafraid)? Explain.

- ☐ Yes
- ☐ No

For Him and Her. Compare your responses. Strive to actively listen to your spouse, so you can better understand what he/she is trying to tell you. People often spend lots of time and energy building façades to hide the "truth" because they are afraid of something. So, take your time to demonstrate a *true transparency* in your relationship that will put you on the path to total and complete "oneness" with each other.

Father,

Your Word says, "The truth shall set you free, confess your sins to each other, and pray for each other, so you may be healed." Father, I ask you right now for the courage to speak my 'truths' to my spouse. Help me see each day, as an opportunity to be both honest and loving. Help my spouse and me become two vessels determined to give more than we are given. I thank you, Father, because my growth and healing are in my 'truth.' In Jesus Name, Amen.

SESSION SIX

Session Six will focus on Chapter Six, *Loving Your Spouse*. In this chapter, Dr. Sanders debunks the myth of falling in and out of love, and explains how *love is a choice*. She also discusses the importance of embracing marriage, as a spiritual relationship and biblical scriptures that will help grow your love and your marriage. To prepare for this session, read Chapter Six, in its entirety. Remember, answer the general questions first, and then the questions that pertain to your specific gender. In addition to the general questions and gender specific questions, couples should answer the questions designated for him and her.

The scriptures accompanying this section are:

1 Corinthians
Genesis 2: 18-24
Ephesians 5:21

Isaiah 54:17
James 1:19-20

*Continue to journal your thoughts and any notes in Appendix F.

CHAPTER SIX
LOVING YOUR SPOUSE
QUESTIONS

This chapter opens up with a common statement that is often misused, "You can't help who you fall in love with." Dr. Sanders debunks this myth by explaining that love is not only a feeling, but also a decision - one that involves sacrifice, selflessness, and transformation. When you embrace love as a *choice*, it becomes an "attitude" that requires strength and humility. Strength and humility that is only possible with God's help. And, although there may be times when you think your spouse is being cold and unloving towards you, it is important to *choose love*. A *choice* that requires hard work like listening, when it's easier to blame, choosing to stay, when it's easier to walk away, choosing to forgive, when it's easier to hold a grudge, choosing to comfort, when the world tells you to turn your back, choosing to support, when you have been burned, choosing to be honest, when it's easier to lie, and lastly, choosing to be selfless, when you could be selfish. Learning to love your spouse is essential to allowing God's plan for marriage to manifest in your marriage.

How have you *allowed* love to become a *choice* in your marriage?

_____

_____

_____

_____

_____

_____

_____

_____

For Him: To embrace love as a *choice* and adopt an "attitude" of love, ask your spouse these questions:

1. What can I do to help you?

2. How can I be a better husband to you?

3. What can I do to make your life easier?

For Her: To embrace love as a *choice* and adopt an "attitude" of love, ask your spouse these questions:

1. What can I do to help you?

2. How can I be a better wife to you?

3. What can I do to make your life easier?

For Him and Her: The questions in this section are designed to help you choose love and embrace an "attitude" of love. Note: It's important to implement what you learn from the "Him" and "Her" sections on a regular basis, regardless of your spouse's responses.

Change your attitude and behaviors, so they truly reflect love as a choice. If possible, further the discussion by asking your spouse additional questions.

On pgs. 77-78, Dr. Sanders explores both the "I" perspective and the "we" perspective. When you focus on the "I" perspective instead of the "we" perspective, you prevent God's plan from manifesting in your marriage.

What are you doing to incorporate more of the "we" perspective (instead of the "I" perspective) into your marriage?

_____
_____
_____
_____
_____
_____
_____
_____
_____
_____
_____
_____
_____
_____

No one is *perfect*, therefore, do not expect your marriage to be *perfect*. In other words, do not be alarmed by the disagreements that arise in your marriage – just be prepared. *Prepared to focus on the problem solver (God) and not the problem.*

On pg. 80, Dr. Sanders provides tips that have helped her resolve conflict in her own marriage. How do you handle disagreements in your marriage? Check all that apply.

- ☐ Humble yourself before God, and ask Him to reveal what you contributed to the disagreement or conflict.
- ☐ Confess your anger to God before confronting your spouse.
- ☐ Ask God for forgiveness for your part in the disagreement or conflict.
- ☐ Thank God for His forgiveness. And, be willing to seek forgiveness from your spouse, and grant forgiveness to your spouse.
- ☐ Allow your spouse to speak freely without shifting blame and vice versa.
- ☐ Listen to your spouse and encourage him/her to listen to you. And, strive to understand your spouse's perspective, instead of convincing your spouse to understand yours.
- ☐ Tell the truth.
- ☐ Do not leave a disagreement or conflict unresolved.
- ☐ Discuss one issue at a time.
- ☐ Other

How do you contribute to disagreements in your marriage?

_____
_____
_____
_____
_____
_____
_____

_____
_____
_____
_____
_____
_____

During disagreements, what are you most likely to say?

- ☐ You do not listen to me.

  -or-

- ☐ I do not *feel* like you are listening to me.

For Him: How can you improve the way you address conflict in your marriage?

_____
_____
_____
_____
_____
_____
_____
_____
_____

For Her. How can you improve the way you address conflict in your marriage?

_____
_____
_____
_____
_____
_____
_____
_____
_____
_____
_____
_____

For Him and Her. Discuss your responses with your spouse, and think of areas you commonly disagree on, such as: finances, roles and responsibilities, in-laws, parenting, intimacy, and others. This will help you identify unresolved or reoccurring conflicts that have hurt your marriage or spouse. It also helps to identify areas where growth is needed.

Heavenly Father,
I know I cannot be the spouse you want me to be without your help. So, help me love my spouse in the same way that you show love to me. Stop me from keeping a record of 'wrongs.' Today, I release my marriage to you, choosing love, instead of anger and resentment. Father, please allow me to be sensitive to your voice, so I can receive all of your guidance and blessings. In Jesus Name, Amen.

SESSION SEVEN

Session Seven focuses on Chapter Seven, *Growing Your Love God's Way*. In this chapter, Dr. Sanders explains the importance of growing your love *God's way* and continues the discussion about *love being a choice*. This chapter will help you better understand if you want to love your spouse with God's love, being spiritually connected to both Him and your spouse is vital. To prepare for this session, read Chapter Seven, in its entirety. Remember, answer the general questions first, then the questions that pertain to your specific gender. In addition to the general questions and gender specific questions, couples should answer the questions designated for him and her.

The scriptures accompanying this section are:

Jeremiah 29:11
Malachi 2:13-16
Genesis 2:18-24

Romans 12:2
2 Corinthians 10:5
1 Corinthians 13:4-8

Continue to journal your thoughts and any notes in Appendix G.

Chapter Seven
Growing Your Love God's Way
Questions

On pg. 83, Dr. Sanders continues the discussion about choosing to love her spouse. The difficulty of this choice is expressed as Dr. Sanders discusses her life experience regarding this matter.

What are your thoughts about the statement "choosing to love your spouse is or can be difficult?"

_____
_____
_____
_____
_____
_____
_____
_____
_____
_____
_____
_____
_____

For Him and Her: Share your responses with your spouse. Talk about each other's thoughts and feelings.

Continuing on pg. 84, Dr. Sanders admits that she allowed many issues from her past that had never been addressed to impact her attitude, behavior, beliefs, and values. Those issue became the fabric of her being, and her marriage reflected what she believed to be the truth at the time.

Where did your attitude, behavior, beliefs, and values on marriage come from? Check all that apply.

- ☐ Family
- ☐ Other Married Couples
- ☐ Peers
- ☐ Workforce
- ☐ Social Influences
- ☐ Life Experiences (divorce, past relationships, trauma, etc.)
- ☐ Religion
- ☐ Media (music, T.V., social media, etc.)
- ☐ Culture

Of the sources you checked, how have you allowed them to impact your behavior towards you spouse and your marriage, both positively and negatively?

_____
_____
_____
_____
_____
_____
_____
_____
_____
_____

For Him and Her: Discuss your responses with your spouse. Determine how you and your spouse can change negative attitudes, behaviors, beliefs, and values on marriage into positive ones.

On pg. 85, Dr. Sanders describes a point in time when she recognized the need to choose love.

Have you ever found yourself saying I do not think I love my spouse anymore?

- ☐ Yes
- ☐ No

If your response was "Yes," it's "Ok." Growing your love with your spouse means choosing love daily and it requires God's help. As discussed in the previous section, choosing love means constantly reminding yourself of God's plan for marriage which can be found in Jeremiah 29:11, Malachi 2:13–16, and Genesis 2:18–24. It also means changing the way you respond to your spouse's concerns and issues (renewing your mind). Therefore, make a choice daily to choose to love your spouse. Every day will not be easy, and there will be some days when you do not think your spouse is being very loveable. But, you must remember you have control over your thoughts and the choices you make.

For Him and Her: Discuss your response with your spouse. Be transparent, listen for understanding, and be sensitive to your spouse's response. This question will better help you understand your spouse's concerns.

Dear Father,
I thank you for my spouse. Help us draw closer to you, so our love will continue to grow in your name. Father, today, I let go of past hurts, leaving them in the past. I ask that you make your plan for our marriage clear and evident. Show us what marriage can be with you in the center of it. In Jesus Name, Amen.

SESSION EIGHT

Congratulations! You are almost there. Session Eight is your last session. So far you have learned about God's plan for marriage, discussed the foundation of your marriage, learned about the "vicious cycle," addressed some issues that you have ignored in your marriage, confessed your truth to your spouse through transparency, learned how love is a choice, and began to implement the choice of love. In this session, you will cover Chapter Eight *Tips For Growing Your Love God's Way*, in which you will discover eleven insights needed to grow your love and rebuild your marriage on a new foundation strengthened by God's love. These insights are backed by biblical scriptures and provide a guide to obtaining God's promise for marriage. Remember, to prepare for this session be sure to read Chapter Eight in its entirety. Also remember, everyone taking the *Growing Your Love Journey* should answer the general questions first and the questions that apply to your gender. In addition to the general questions and gender specific questions, couples should answer the questions designated for him and her.

The scriptures that accompany this section are:

Romans 12:10
Colossians 3:19
Proverbs 21:19
1 Corinthians 13:4-8
Song of Solomon 2:10
Proverbs 4:23
Proverbs 27:17
Proverbs 15:1

James 1:19-20
James 5:16
Proverbs 19:11
Ephesians 4:32
Ephesians 4:26-27
Matthew 19:6
Proverbs 3:6
James 1:5

Mark 3:25
Hebrews 13:4
Genesis 2:24

1 Peter 5:7
Psalm 55:22
Acts 10:34

*Continue to journal your thoughts and any notes in Appendix G.

Chapter Eight
Tips For Growing Your Love God's Way
Questions

In a nutshell, Dr. Sanders makes it clear and simple by stating that although there is no one-size-fits-all plan for a happy and successful marriage, the Word should be used, as your guide to assist you in building a stronger relationship with both your spouse and with God.

Tip 1: "Make it Your Primary Goal in Your Marriage to Make Your Spouse Happy" is found on pg. 90. When you put your spouse first and place his/her needs above your own, you are serving God. You can also accomplish this goal by spending quality time with your spouse and doing things that make him/her happy.

What has caused you to unintentionally neglect your spouse? Check all that apply.

- ☐ Peers
- ☐ Work
- ☐ Children
- ☐ Family
- ☐ Technology & Electronics
- ☐ Education
- ☐ Personal Interests (Hobbies)
- ☐ Entertainment
- ☐ Other _____

For Him: In what ways can you put your wife first?

_____
_____
_____

For Her: In what ways can you put your husband first?

For Him and Her: Remember, the time you spend together should be "us" time. As described in the book, "us" time is designated just for you and your spouse – no one or nothing else. Discuss your responses and think of ways to have more "us" time with your spouse. Put your spouse first, learn what makes him/her happy - not just what you feel should make him/her happy.

According to Dr. Sanders, connecting with your spouse, throughout the day, while you are apart, makes the time you have together, when you reconnect more *meaningful*. Do you connect with your spouse, during the day, when you are away from each other?

- ☐ Yes
- ☐ No
- ☐ Sometimes

List two ways you can better connect with your spouse throughout the day? Refer to pg. 91 for examples.

1.

2.

For Him and Her. Putting your spouse first, spending "us" time together, and connecting with your spouse throughout the day will help you build a closer relationship with him/her. Remember, your spouse is the one person who has promised to love you unconditionally, regardless of any circumstance. Therefore, you should appreciate him/her more than anyone else. Discuss your response with your spouse, and make a commitment to put each other first.

Tip 2: "Love and Respect Your Spouse" can be found on pg. 91. The words *love* and *respect* are both verbs and nouns. Therefore, by definition, *action* and an *attitude* are required. *Mutual love and respect are essential for a strong healthy marriage.* Husbands love their wives by respecting them, and wives respect their husbands by loving them. To sum it up, husbands are to love their wives and wives are to respect their husbands. To better understand the importance of loving and respecting your spouse, one must have an understanding of the role of husbands and the role of wives, as found in Ephesians 5:21-33. More information can be found in Session Three and Session Four.

For Him: I show love for my wife by…

___

For Her: I am respectful to my husband by…

For Him: I can be cold and unloving towards my wife by…

For Her: I can be disrespectful towards my husband by…

For Him and Her: Compare your answers, and discuss what it means to *love* and *respect* each other. As Dr. Sanders mentioned on pg. 93, do not get too caught up in trying to "change" your spouse because only

God can do that. Therefore, the only thing you can do is love and respect him/her for who he/she is.

Tip 3: "Do Not be Afraid of Change and Court Your Spouse" can be found on pg. 94. Trying new things with your spouse can help decrease boredom, bring you closer together as a couple, and make you feel a whole lot happier and more satisfied in your marriage.

Have you ever found yourself saying, "Let's do something different?"

- ☐ Yes
- ☐ No
- ☐ Not Really
- ☐ Sometime

List three new things you would like to try with your spouse.

1.

2.

3.

For Him and Her: Discuss your responses with your spouse and make a commitment to implement a least one of the new things you mentioned throughout the week.

Tip 4: "Appreciate Your Spouse" can be found on pg. 94. This tip will help you better understand why it is important to foster gratitude and appreciation. FYI: Saying "Thank you" for little things will go a long way in your marriage. It will also make your spouse feel like you appreciate him/her more. Moreover, do not keep score of who did what and when, because it will only weaken the bond you have built with your spouse.

How often do you tell your spouse "Thank you" before finding fault?

- ☐ Frequently
- ☐ Sometimes
- ☐ Rarely

For Him: I would like my wife to show her appreciation to me by…

___

For Her: I would like my husband to show his appreciation to me by…

___

_____
_____
_____
_____
_____
_____
_____
_____
_____

For Him and Her: Review your responses with your spouse, and notate *three* things you'll commit to doing in the next week to show your spouse your gratitude and appreciation.

1.

2.

3.

Tip 5: "Invest in Your Marriage" can be found on pg. 98. In this chapter, you will learn that it does not matter how long you have been married, be it 10 months or 10 years, you can always become a better spouse. And, because most of us are not trained on how to become a better spouse, investing in your marriage will show you how to do just that.

What have you done to invest in your marriage? Check all that apply.

- ☐ Pray with and for your spouse daily
- ☐ Attend church together regularly
- ☐ Purchase and review marriage-building materials (i.e. books, videos, workbooks, etc.)
- ☐ Attend marriage retreats, conferences, and seminars
- ☐ Flirt with your spouse, as if you are dating
- ☐ Actively listen when your spouse speaks
- ☐ Serve your spouse (by performing "selfless" acts)
- ☐ Other _____

Based on your response to the previous question, what areas do you need to improve, in order to better invest in your marriage?

_____
_____
_____
_____
_____
_____
_____
_____
_____

For Him and Her: Discuss your responses to the previous questions. Note: Investing in your marriage requires giving something to it, rather than taking something away from it. This may sound simple, but actually, it requires tremendous thought and discipline because you have to set aside your desires for your spouses.

Moreover, spending time with other married couples, who have *decided* to put God first in their marriages is a great way to grow your love and rebuild your marriage. By surrounding yourself with these "faithful" couples, you can communicate with them as to how they have managed to maintain a strong marriage through "trials and tribulations." You are also better able to observe how these couples speak to and interact with each other. Note: Refrain from surrounding yourself with individuals, who are always complaining about their spouses.

For Him: Complete the following statement: "I invest in my wife by…" Check all that apply.

- ☐ Making her a top priority after God (not giving your spouse your leftover time)
- ☐ Setting aside your desire to be "right"
- ☐ Helping her grow spiritually
- ☐ Honoring her
- ☐ *Choosing* to love when you do not feel like it
- ☐ Protecting her
- ☐ Other _____

For Her: Complete the following statement: "I invest in my husband by…" Check all that apply.

- ☐ Making him a top priority after God (not giving your spouse your leftover time)
- ☐ Setting aside your desire to be "right"
- ☐ Helping him grow spiritually
- ☐ Respecting him
- ☐ *Choosing* to love when you do not feel like it
- ☐ Supporting him
- ☐ Other _____

Tip 6: "Mastering the Art of Listening" can be found on pg. 100. *Active listening* is the most important tool in effective communication because effective communication requires the art of active listening. Effective communication only occurs when there is a clear understanding of what is being said on both ends. When you really begin to listen, you become better equipped to deal with issues that would, otherwise, do more harm than good.

When communicating with your spouse how do you normally respond?

- ☐ Listen to respond

    -or-

- ☐ Listen for understanding

Many couples are often too busy to actively listen to each because there is always something else that has to get done.

Have you fallen into this trap?

- ☐ Yes
- ☐ No

For Him: I can become a better listener by… Check all that apply.

- ☐ Decreasing any distractions
- ☐ Listening for understanding, not just to respond
- ☐ Seeking to understand my wife's perspective
- ☐ Letting my wife finish her complete thought before I interrupt
- ☐ Checking my attitude
- ☐ Acknowledging what is being said
- ☐ Responding to what my spouse is saying or asking - not giving unsolicited advice

For Her: I can become a better listener by… Check all that apply.

- ☐ Decreasing distractions
- ☐ Listening for understanding, not just to respond
- ☐ Seeking to understand my husband's perspective
- ☐ Letting my husband finish his complete thought before I interrupt
- ☐ Checking my attitude
- ☐ Acknowledging what is being said
- ☐ Responding to what my spouse is saying or asking - not giving unsolicited advice

For Him and Her: Begin implementing some of the responses you checked throughout the week. Observe the impact, and journal your observations in the "Notes Section."

Tip 7: "Resolve Conflict and Forget It" can be found on pg. 101. *Conflict resolution cannot be done without effective communication.* While marital conflict is common, conflict is a good tool to strengthen your relationship, because it tests your faith. The challenge is, however, to learn how to properly address conflict in a way that is beneficial to your marriage.

How do you respond to conflict in your marriage?

- ☐ Sarcasm
- ☐ Cold Shoulder
- ☐ Pretending that no conflict exists
- ☐ Withdrawal
- ☐ Discussions *after* you and your spouse have had time to calm down and think
- ☐ Yelling
- ☐ Nagging
- ☐ Discussing heated issues in the moment
- ☐ Giving in

For Him and Her. Refer to pg. 80 for tips on how to handle conflict and review your response on how to improve the way you handle conflict (workbook pg. 80).

"Letting go" is an integral part of forgiveness. If you find yourself saying, "Remember, when you said [blah blah blah] ... I did not like that, and I feel [blah blah blah] ..." after you have come to a resolution on an issue, as Dr. Sanders mentions on pg. 103, then you have not truly forgiven your spouse. In other words, you have not "let go" of the issue. "True forgiveness" is a choice. A choice that requires you to "give up" the desire to be right. "Let go" of the issue! And, before bringing up an issue after it has been addressed, ask yourself the following questions.

1. Is it really worth it?
2. Is my spouse more important than this issue?
3. Am I willing to put additional time and effort into addressing this issue again?
4. Will talking about this issue again change the outcome of the resolution?

If you answered, "No," to all of these questions, then "let it go." However, if you answered, "Yes," to at least two of these questions, then, address the issue to seek resolution, using a variety of tactics. Note: Simply sharing your concerns usually works best.

Tip 8: "Keep Christ at the Center of Your Marriage and Pray with Your Spouse" can be found on pg. 104. In a "Christ-centered" marriage, God is *first* - not your spouse, money, concerns and issues, or even material things. A "Christ-centered" marriage offers guidance, as God's Word is the cure for restoring love and happiness. Oftentimes, couples say they have a "Christ-centered" marriage, but in reality, they have not given God total control of their lives, and thus, are not allowing the Holy Spirit to guide and empower them. Have you truly given God total control, so you can have a "Christ-centered" marriage?

☐ Yes
☐ No

How often do you and your spouse pray, read, study the Word, and attend church together?

- ☐ Frequently
- ☐ Sometimes
- ☐ Rarely

A few ways to promote a "Christ-centered" marriage include: making prayer a priority by praying with your spouse and for your spouse, dedicating time to come together, as a couple before Christ, developing an individual relationship with God, and embracing, believing, and acting on God's plan for marriage. In what areas do you need to make improvements? Compare your response with your spouse, and make a commitment to foster a "Christ-centered" marriage.

_____
_____
_____
_____
_____
_____
_____
_____
_____
_____
_____
_____

Tip 9: "Discuss Financial Matters' can be found on pg. 106. *Financial discord is one of the top relationship stressors.* Thus, developing a team approach is important. Oftentimes, financial disagreements occur because both parties do not truly understand how to use the money.

What do you call the funds that both you and your spouse have?

- ☐ Mine and Yours

    -or-

- ☐ Ours

Developing an approach to handle finances is essential for walking in unity with your spouse. This means, putting together a plan for who handles the finances and how, creating a monthly budget, developing a strategy for saving and investing, and a making a plan for giving back to God.

What is your approach to handling finances?

_____
_____
_____
_____
_____
_____
_____
_____
_____
_____
_____
_____

Are you and your spouse in agreement with how finances are handled?

    ☐ Yes
    ☐ No

List two ways you can better handle finances:

1.

2.

For Him and Her: Remember, God is the only one who supplies all our needs. It does not matter who earns the most money, you both make a contribution and finances should be decided together. If you have not done so already develop a plan for handling your money and finances that you both can agree on.

Tip 10 "Talk About Your Intimacy Needs" is found on pg. 107. Intimacy with your spouse is not only about sex, however it is necessary to have a conversation about what happens between the sheets. As Dr. Sanders specifies "true intimacy is built on commitment, passion, companionship, and spirituality."

What areas are important to you when it comes down to sexual intimacy? Check all that apply

    ☐ How frequent you have sex
    ☐ Emotional connection
    ☐ Non-sexual touch throughout the day
    ☐ The way in which you verbalize and display love and affection
    ☐ How much time you spend together outside the bedroom
    ☐ Foreplay before sex

For Him: Of the areas listed above what area(s) would you like your wife to improve in?

_____
_____
_____

For Her: Of the areas listed above what area(s) would you like your husband to improve in?

_____
_____
_____

For Him and Her: Compare your responses, as these questions will help you become open about your sexual intimacy needs. It will also help you better understand the needs of your spouse. When commitment, passion, companionship, and spiritual intimacy is missing, sex with your spouse can quickly become boring, routine, and self-focused, which means it loses its depth.

What can you do to strengthen these areas in your marriage? Refer to pg. 109 to review characteristics of these four factors.

_____
_____
_____
_____
_____
_____

_____
_____
_____
_____
_____
_____
_____

Tip 11: "Keep Your Issues in Your Marriage" can be found on pg. 109. Simply put, your marital issues cannot and should not be shared with everyone.

Who do you seek help from when you have marital issues?

- ☐ Parents
- ☐ In-laws
- ☐ Family members (i.e. sister, brother, aunt, uncle, etc.)
- ☐ Pastor, minister, spiritual mentor, or marriage counselor
- ☐ Friends
- ☐ Co-workers
- ☐ God

For Him and Her: Share your response with your spouse, and discuss how your confidants have impacted your relationship. Allow God to be your problem-solver, taking all of your problems to Him first. If you need further guidance, seek help from your Pastor, minister, spiritual mentor, or marriage counselor.

While it is okay to talk about marriage, in general, with other people, it is not okay to discuss your marital issues with everyone. In fact, it can be very disrespectful to your spouse, increasing the likelihood that your spouse will feel betrayed. Plus, others may start to view him/her in a different way. Most likely the person, who you are confiding in is concerned more about you than your marriage.

Bonus Tip 12: "Love Yourself"

Before entering into marriage, it is essential to know who you are in order to love yourself. In the event that you missed this step, and you find yourself in a marriage…do not worry, you can still learn to love yourself. Like Dr. Sanders, sometimes people enter into marriage not knowing who they are and not loving themselves, thinking it is the responsibility of their spouse to fill that empty space. Not true! Not knowing who you are and not loving yourself can lead to difficulty in *choosing* to love your spouse. Loving yourself means knowing who you are in Christ, and being thankful and appreciative of the person God made you to be. It does not mean being arrogant, prideful, and full of self-worship. When you take on the arrogant, prideful, and self-worship type of love; self-hatred, bitterness toward oneself, low self-esteem, self-rejection, and being ashamed of yourself become symptoms. This can and will cause loving your spouse to become extremely difficult. However, because you were created in God's image, you must remember that you are fearfully and wonderfully made. Therefore, learning to love yourself means understanding who you are in Christ. This sentiment is underscored or pg. 22.

> *I will praise thee; for I am fearfully and wonderfully made: marvelous are thy works; and that my soul knoweth right well. (Psalms 139:14 [KJV])*
>
> *And God said, Let us make man in our image, after our likeness… (Genesis 1:26 [KJV])*

Father,
I thank you in advance for the growth in my marriage, as my spouse and I embark on this spirit-filled journey. I thank you for making our marriage a testimony of our faith. Father, as I implement strategies I've learned on this journey, please cover me, my spouse, and my marriage in your omnipresent light and grace. Today, I immerse myself in the amour of God, ever ready to go to war for my marriage, because the enemy cannot and will not destroy what you have put together. Father, give me the strength to stand firm against tactics that strive to destroy our union, the wisdom to make good decisions, and the desire to be more selfless. Continue to mold my spouse and me into who you have destined for us to be. In Jesus Name, Amen.

Growing Your Love Pledge

I _____ *choose* love. I *choose* you. I *choose* to put God at the center of our marriage and seek him for guidance in every area of our marriage. Today, I pledge and *choose* to love daily, to work diligently, to listen, instead of blame, to stay, when it's easier to walk away, to forgive, when it's easier to hold a grudge, to comfort, when the world tells me to turn my back, to support, when I have been burned, to be honest, when it's easier to lie, and most importantly to be selfless, when I could be selfish.

For Husbands:
As a husband, I *choose* to love and cherish you just as Christ loves the church. I pledge to pray with you and for you, always strengthening and encouraging you.

For Wives:
As a wife, I *choose* to respect you just, as God tells me to. I pledge to pray with you and for you, always strengthening and encouraging you.

_____
Husband Signature

_____
Wife Signature

_____
Date

Session One Notes
Appendix A

Session Two Notes
Appendix B

Session Three Notes
Appendix C

Session Four Notes
Appendix D

Session Five Notes
Appendix E

Session Six Notes
Appendix F

Session Seven Notes
Appendix G

Session Eight Notes
Appendix H

About The Author

Dr. Shameka Mack Sanders was raised in St. George, South Carolina, and graduated from Cappella University with top honors. She worked in education for five years before starting Sanders Publications, a company dedicated to guiding clients through the self-publishing process.

Dr. Sanders was inspired to write *Growing Your Love After The "I Do's" God's Way,* after experiencing firsthand how the word of God strengthened and transformed her own marriage. Dr. Sanders is also a prolific self-help and children's author.

Growing Your Love After The "I Do's" God's Way Workbook

Dr. Shameka Mack Sanders

Made in the USA
Columbia, SC
25 September 2017